TWILIGHT OF THE DICTATORS

POEMS OF TYRANNY AND LIBERATION
by
BRETT RUTHERFORD &
PIETER VANDERBECK

Second edition, expanded

With illustrations by
Pieter Vanderbeck

THE POET'S PRESS
Pittsburgh, PA

ISBN 0-922558-39-6
This book also published in
Adobe Acrobat format.

This is the 180th publication of
THE POET'S PRESS
2209 Murray Avenue #3 / Pittsburgh PA 15217
www.poetspress.org

TABLE OF CONTENTS

MILLENNIAL WINDS

HOW THIS BOOK CAME TO BE

APPENDIX

DARK
YEARS

THINGS COULD GO BADLY FOR YOU.

Pieter Vanderbeck

THE COLLABORATOR

Yes, I am a collaborator:
   that's what I am!
   And I'll tell you something else:
   I'm proud!
   Yes, proud!

I am respected!
Respected by the right people!
The ones who count!
Who are you?
Look at yourself!
Ridiculed! Laughed at!
No one listens to you!
But *me?* —
I ride on the knife-edge of history!
Every word I say has consequence!
My thoughts are visible to the mass!
I am but the electrode of public opinion!
No one calls me an enemy!
I am loved by all!
Do you know what they call you?
I did not want to tell you.
I did not want to hurt your feelings.
But I must, if anyone.
You have gone too far.
You need to be shocked into recognizance,
harshly and energetically.
This is for your own good.
What they say:
you are a crank,
a person who lives only in his own world,
infecting others with your own irrelevant problems,
fooling people into liking you,
being grateful to you, and thinking you are good.

They will hate you all the more,
when they realize they have been fooled,
that you put the voodoo on them!

You will be torn to pieces!
I tell you this for your health.
You may be too far gone to recant:
no one can forget what you did.
But at least get out of the way,
and let progress march on.

Look at me!
I have bread on the table!
No one calls me any names!
I am respected, loved.
I have security,
every morning and every night.
I can sleep well.
Yes,
sleep well.
I listen for no knock on the door.
I know I am here,
and will remain here.
I can feel good about myself.
I have a pure heart and a clean conscience!

Look at yourself!
Do you think what anyone else thinks?
No!
That's the harsh answer:
certainly no!
All your own thoughts that you made up yourself!
Can you call that objective reality?
Be honest!
You infect the universe with things that are not real!
Look at the stars in the sky!
They smile on me, not you!
The fates are with me!
Destiny is with me!
Because I am with destiny!

I represent the people!
I say what they think!
And what I say,
they think!
All you have
is a small circle of doomed ...
of doomed ...
of doomed misfits, detritus, scraps, garbage, filth!
They will go down with you,
and be forgotten!
Or realize,
and tear you to bits!
Wise up, infection!
You should know where you are!
I know you have some potential for reason!
I know you are not as mad as you pretend!
You cannot fool me!
I know you are conscious of the way things are!
That is all can say.
Your oblivion, your misery, is all your own calling,
it falls on your own head.
I cannot help you.
You are beyond redemption.
These are the last words
you will ever hear from the voice of society!

Brett Rutherford

IVAN GROZNI

Ivan Grozni,
    Tyrant of the Oprichniks
Little Father to the trembling serfs.
Your murders pale, poor Ivan the Terrible,
beside the deeds of a fat old man —
a pensioned auto worker
    front porch grandpa in old Cleveland
a beer and pretzel neighbor
    picnics and barbecues
    ball games on the radio
nodding to sleep before the television.

He is another Ivan, *Ivan Grozni,*
Ivan the Terrible
            lord of Treblinka
counting the days to his
              Social Security check,
his numbered entitlement —

As Ivan he numbered his subjects —
gypsies and Jews and misfits,
counted them by the hundred,
gassed them by the thousand,
bookkeeping entries at every
      ten thousand mark,
medal from the Fuhrer
      for every tenth
      of a million exterminated,
numbers on a golden arch of death

Gold watch retirement gift —
good man on the assembly line,
speedy with wrench and rivet —
how many cars did he finish?
A mere few thousand, maybe,
      nothing to match

the nine hundred thousand
     he prodded in
     through the one-way door.
He understood efficiency.
     Their slouching gait
     from off the boxcars
     not fast enough,
he whipped and prodded,
maimed and mowed down
the laggards and lame ones.

(His fat hands picked out
     the defective bolts,
dropped them to bin —
nobody's business where
  they went —)

Tried for his crimes
he rallies his wife and family,
hires an attorney to fight
this case of mistaken identity.
He smiles at the battered old Jews
who say they remember him,
call him the Beast of Treblinka,
waves to the courtroom audience
and says in Hebrew —
                           I am innocent.
I am not Ivan the Terrible.

Yet who are these ghosts
that crowd the air,
clotting the room with accusation?
Who are these legion whisperers,
nine tenths of a million strong
chanting like monks at a Tsar's interment
singing like bells of monotonous iron
one steeple truth in a landscape of lies:

Ivan .... Ivan .... Ivan Grozni.

Pieter Vanderbeck

BORDER GUARD

The border guard mans his station by the dotted line.
    It is on all maps; it is there.
On some, the lines are a mile long.
On larger scales, the lines are a hundred feet.
On world maps, they can be many, many miles.
But it is all the same:
a certain latitude, in reality a long unbroken line.
And it is all his.
Some others have longitudes.

His station is the only one between his two horizons.
A little wooden shack,
square at the corners,
angled at the roof.
From that roof there runs a telephone line.
He can call any other booth.
Every booth together can call...
Central Control.
At Central, there is air conditioning,
fluorescent lighting fixtures on the ceiling,
more than one room, with doors opening between them,
a number of personnel under a grand supervisor,
and ... and ...
the biggest radio set of them all,
accompanied by its own separate broadcasting tower!

He hungers for promotion;
but, as in everything, there are pros and cons.
He has his own booth.
And there, he has absolute control.
Any organic carbon form that crosses over,
he can do anything with he likes.
If an inorganic carbon form somehow rolls across,
then he can throw it back.
He has it made.

A dotted line,
a booth,
proper implements,
his weekly pay,
and various perks:
a weekend for a good time,
all the booze he wants,
possession of all he can confiscate,
and a four-wheel vehicle provided free,
including gas.

A place in life,
responsibilities,
power;
he's made it!

Brett Rutherford

SOLZHENITSYN IN NEW YORK,
AT THE BOLSHOI OPERA

A spectre is haunting
the orchestra.
Bolshoi Opera
at Lincoln Center
on its New York visit;
exile in his seat,
down from his Vermont
dacha for a slice of
Mussorgsky's Old Russia.

Onstage, the false Dmitri,
a mad young monk
who believes himself
the murdered Tsarevich
restored by miracle to life,
approaches his destiny —

the guilty Tsar clock-shrieks,
the impossibility
of the boy he already killed —
an impossible boy
whose rebel army advances
now upon the Kremlin.

How can such things be?
The dead must be commanded
to stay that way! A former person
cannot become a person again!
We have erased his name
from the history books!

Each throb of pendulum
heart-hammers him:
I killed you I'm coming
I saw you dead — An old man
saw me risen. The Poles
have already acknowledged me.

Usurper, imposter, ghost!
What use are borders,
what consolation exile
when they *come back*?

At break of act
the singers —
the dark-eyed Boris,
the blond Dmitri,
the hermit monk Pimen,
the Polish seductress,
scan darkened aisles
for one glimpse
of Alexandr Isaievich
whose name
        they are not allowed to utter
whose books
        they are not allowed to read

the novelist
a bristling field of names
a nation émigré in one,
a walking catalog
of uncountable deaths
on steppe and taiga.

You're dead,
the Kremlin telegrams.
I'm here, the exile
reminds his enemies.
One day I'll be *there*.
The held-in-check
will be checkmate.

Later Mussorgsky's
tyrant dies,
invoking god,
anointing a child tsar
to follow him:

I am still Tsar!
Ya Tsar yeshcho!
Boris falls dead
as tyrants must.
A truth-cloud waits.
It has all time to attend
to its business.
It will not let them sleep.

Pieter Vanderbeck

SITTING IN MY APARTMENT WITH COLD SOAKED FEET ON A HEAVILY OVERCAST DAY RAINING WITH SLUSH BORDERING ON SNOW IN A BAD MOOD HAVING LOOKED THROUGH A *NATIONAL GEOGRAPHIC* PICTURE ARTICLE ON DAILY LIFE IN EAST BERLIN

In the Leninplatz
they walk through constant slush
waiting for no bus that will come
but not acknowledging that it isn't there
waiting in groups of no more than two
and not speaking to each other
going to the state apartment
with one light burning on the staircase
one light in the room
a pan of ascetic stew on the hotplate
and a single blanket and sheet on the bed
that doubles as a sofa
though there are no guests to entertain
because everyone is staying in
and only the People's Democratic Police are out watching
all fulfilling the glory of the Marxist dream.

On the second floor of the
Ministry of Internal Harmony
the grand staircase
lighted by one utilitarian bulb
is a steel-beam affair
climbing up surreptitiously in one corner
to hidden place after hidden place
from Eight-Cee to Eight-Dee to Eight-Ee

where the office of the Mayor
a popular luminary
is lit by one spare bulb
on a rubber cord

with a pull string
and without a shade
over the big wooden desk
where he sits
with a teacup
and a thin tea bag
in lukewarm water
because hot is extravagant
and not coffee because that is decadent
and even on state visits refuses coffee out of disgust
and out the window
the pitter-patter of Marxist sleet
on the empty abandoned square
with one person being watched and one person watching.

It was this way last year
this way last decade
it will be
this way next year
this way next decade
all decades are the same decade
there is only one decade
there is no other decade
yesterday's newspaper is today's newspaper
and there was never anything but stew.

Excitement flashes across the horizon
the periodic
monthly or yearly
(don't ask which)
sports rally
showing the pinnacle of Marxist development
without equal
for there is no competing team
there is but one team
the winning team
come and cheer and clap and exult and rejoice
and be observed being there

so there will not be that slip of reprimand at the office
begging to come to the supervisor's office
for a friendly and thoughtful chat
over a thin tea
under a single bulb
while it rains sleet outside.

STALIN AND SHOSTAKOVICH

It's three in the morning and snowing in Moscow.
The streets are dark — but here and there a light —
a solitary bulb throws out its beacon:
a yellow beam from Stalin's workroom,
steady when the Great Helmsman has an idea,
tilted downward as he studies his lists,
casting a shadow of his giant hand
   as fountain pen
makes check marks next to offending names.
Tomorrow those names and their owners
will separate forever as People's Enemies
become "Former People."
The offices of Ministries are well lit, too —
memos to write, conspiracies to ferret out,
coffee to drain by the cup, by the gallon.
(If Comrade Stalin can work all night,
who dares to leave his tasks unfinished?)
At the Lubyanka Jail, one basement window
emits its light in slitted segments.
One could see —
if anyone dared to press his face there —
an arm with a truncheon — a mangled visage.
Dim slots of light — a doorway — come on and off.
Men in black coats are framed there.
Then slashing beams and feral taillights
precede and follow the Black Marias.

2
The clock chimes four.
Another lamp is burning, too —
another hand makes nervous tick marks
as Shostakovich blocks out chords and melodies.
Even the vodka and cigarettes
are quite forgotten as the climax approaches.
Eyes blur with staves,
  sharps dance like angry snowflakes.

HE IS STILL THERE.

He cannot concentrate.
　　Half his brain is listening.
　　Not to his inner Muses —
　　　　not tonight,
　　　　not any night this year —
listening for the Black Marias.
A car glides by — too slowly?
Someone is running at the end of the block —
why, at this hour?
An interval of silence — too long, too quiet.
A truck stops — how long
　　until the doors swing wide
　　and heavy-footed steps
　　echo from the building fronts?
A street lamp winks out; across
　　the street a curtain parts,
　　a candle moves once
　　across a table —
is it nothing — or a signal?
He cannot go to the window and look.
Watchers in raincoats
　　dislike being spied upon.
It's never wise to stand in a window, anyway:
　　rocks have been thrown
　　by zealous members of the Communist Youth
　　rocks with notes
　　that read: SHOSTAKOVICH — PARASITE —
　　　　FORMALIST!!!
What if one of them took a gun to a nearby rooftop?
Open season on Formalist Anti-People Artists!
His hands make notes in jagged gesture.
Staccato — staccato — agitato —
Attacca subito —

Stalin condemned his last opera.
What will he think of this symphony —
its Mahleresque, giant orchestra,
its jarring, piled-on harmonies,
its bleak and withering quietudes?
Will this, too, be a "muddle instead of music?"

How can be help being himself?
He writes not what he wants,
    but what he has to.
He tries to be grand — it comes out bombast.
Tries humor, only to ooze sarcasm.
He has no smile that convinces —
could a lobster smile
while dangling over the cooking pot?
He must put everything into this symphony.
It may be his last, anyway.
Ignoring the clock, he labors on.
This page: the whimper of the beaten.
There: the shriek of the victims' widows.
There: the whining voice of the *apparatchik*.
This horn sounds a denunciation.
This oboe betrays a friend for a dacha.
This violin divorces its partner,
disclosing her unacceptable class origins.
A clarinet warns of rootless cosmopolitans.
Let them guess what it's all about!
To hell with their need for uplift!
Rub their faces in the ruin of Russia!
Let them try their dialectic on this one!

3
Stalin works on. He sees the name
of Shostakovich. A memo asks:
Arrest and interrogate?

"I like a tune," he says to himself,
"and now and then even a poem."
The chastised artists would come around.
They'd write their odes and symphonies
to Russia and to Comrade Stalin.
They'd do it willingly.
They'd trample one another for the privilege.
No action at present, the dictator writes.

4
Done for the night, the weary composer
dons coat and shoes, tiptoes
out door to the unheated hall.
Suitcase beside him, he curls up there
between the elevator and the apartment door.
Tries to sleep, tries not to listen
to the spiderweb sounds of the dying night.
The suitcase is packed for a long journey —
        a cold one.
Better to wait in the corridor, he thinks;
better not to wake his sleeping wife and son
if this is the night that makes his life
another unfinished symphony.

Pieter Vanderbeck

MONEY AND BULLETS

Ask the grand scribe of the great book of history
what this Earth represents:
"Alchemy," he says, "The conversion of noble metal into lead."

The Council of Dragons convenes,
in the Important Cities of Noted Nations:
the shining yellow metal they heap into piles before them
upon the oval table of their polymeric concern.
"Power, Gentlemen! The power to prevent men to think.
The capital to manufacture Fear.
Bullets are what we need; and guns to hold them;
    and personnel to man them.
Buy them all!
Steal to buy!
Wring this gold from the lifeblood of destiny!
We must control.
What else are we good for?"
Noble metal!
Wonder of wonder!
The liquid Sun
cast into trinkets
for iron hands to hold.

Culture and Philosophy
held in ransom
by the jealous and false.
Lead for the heart and the brain!
More of it is needed:
ever more,
to reinforce the reinforcements.
Iron bunkers are thrown up.
Borders are closed.

Only the Dragons may come and go as they please.
Only they may raise the shades to see the light of day.
The rest should mind their business.
Their appointed business.
Their organized and planned business.
Where is the gold?
Some of it is still around,
unchecked,
uncharted,
not enrolled in the Central Authority.
Ask the Scribe of History where it is.
"In the Universe, where it always was.
The Dragons cannot go there.
They can freeze the Earth,
but the Sun will shine!"

Brett Rutherford

JUST REWARDS

A Prose Poem

WELCOME TO HEVIN
    a sign in jagged lettering
    nailed to a gap-toothed fence.
Chickens run to and fro on the dirt road.
The smell of manure laces the air.

I must be dreaming.

No dream,
comrade, said an expressionless face
behind wire-rimmed glasses. His
hair was tangled, his T-shirt torn,
his words a snarl of sarcasm and garlic.

It looks like a farm. I thought —

You thought
Heaven would be a city, comrade?
You're in for a few surprises, then.
Things have changed in the Afterlife.
We angels are into collective farming now.
This sector's exclusively potatoes —
you'll be assigned here, until the end
of the current Five Year Plan.

But I hate potatoes. And I've never gardened.

Of course you hate them. That's why you're here.
Just make your quota for a couple years,
maybe you'll work your way up to fresh fruit —
a little shade there, and no digging —
or maybe a clerk's job later if you're lucky.

I didn't think it would be like this —
not for me with a Ph.D. and all —
and all those students I brought around
to class consciousness, my students,
children of the rich!
I mean, am I really dead?

                  Dead
and buried, buster. You bought it,
as the army guys used to say.

But what's going on here? I was GOOD.
I know I preached all this
    was just the opiate for the masses,
but now that I'm here, well,
I was good, wasn't I?
Heaven is reward, not punishment.

OK, fella, let me fill you in on Heaven.
This place used to be a country club, see,
until all the social engineers came along.
The upper classes monopolized God,
Mary threw balls for the Beautiful People,
Jesus and the Saints took care of the poor.
The Arabs and Jews had a bowling league.
The Buddhists chanted, the Hindus built temples.
A lot of people just watched TV and ate,
sometimes four or five generations in a house.

Sounds pretty good to me.

                Well, see that sign?
It says ALL ARE EQUAL BEFORE GOD.
    And see this,
it says ALL POWER TO THE PEOPLE.
    That's the law.

You had a revolution? Here, too?

You got it, comrade. Now God's a pretty generous guy,
most times you want something, you get it.
It happened when all these Marxists arrived.
They weren't quite bad enough for hell,
those Party cranks and college professors,
and not quite good enough to leave things alone.
They were no sooner dead than they started a Party.
They got Socialists and Fabians,
    Wobblies and Anarchists,
    Leninists and Trotskyites,
    Stalinists and Maoists,
    Progressives and Shining Paths.

Now Lenin and Trotsky and Stalin and Marx
aren't here to encourage all this stuff —
they're in the Other Place shoveling ore.
After all, they did kill millions.
But all these ink-stained fellows, they formed a
government, turned God out of his temple,
made Him sulk behind Saturn for a while
until He came back and agreed to share power.

So here's the picture of Paradise. No music,
except maybe the weekly folk-song rally.
The food is some kind of biscuit, not that
you need to eat — it's just a habit.
On Sunday you get potatoes and cabbage soup.
Everyone wears T-shirts and jeans. Men and women
the same. No one uses his old name.
No one gets to see his family or ancestors —

But my wife must be here ... my mother and father ...

Maybe they are, but you're not allowed to find them.
See that poster? FAMILIES PERPETUATE
CLASS OPPRESSION.
You might see your wife at one of the lectures,
the ones for the politically incorrect like you.
But don't let the Secret Angels see you talk to her.

Secret Angels?

Shh — there's one now!
The damn things look like doves, but they're wired.
A Monitor Angel is always listening somewhere.

Are there really angels here? You don't look like one.

I was made one years ago, but I cut the wings
as a gesture of solidarity with the peasants.

I want to see God. I want to protest this.

Suit yourself. You're welcome to try.
He's just down the road — that place with all
the billboards. Look for an old wrecked Ford
and the painting of Comrade Mary, Mother of God,
riding the cab of a harvester. Can't miss it.

Maybe if enough of us talk to God —

Forget it. His Son's in league
with the Communists anyway,
and He gets anything He asks for. But why
complain, man, this is Heaven. For all
its faults it's the place where everyone is equal.

In Hell, they make you work for wages.
In Hell, the geniuses and homosexuals
get all the breaks. Someone's always proving
he's better, more talented.
They wear makeup and design fancy clothes.
They build themselves houses
and tear them down again.
They even have a newspaper called *Hell Today*.
All that foment and striving — no one is ever content
or happy. Man, don't knock it —
It's either this or Hell, and this,
this is the People's Paradise!

Pieter Vanderbeck

BRAWNS 20
BRAINS 0

He lives down the street —
    that writer —
there, alone, in his little house,
the one with all the lights on.
But he is not there.
They know it.

In the bigger building up the street,
with the lights on in only one basement room,
they discuss what to do with him.
He is out at the late night store, they say.
Buying things that are to no good purpose.
And he has to go by there.
They can see him.
They wait, and they discuss.

The cash box is opened.
Ten for you, ten for you,
and ten for you.
There is plenty here, and plenty more.

They are healthy ones.
The healthiest.
A strong body breeds a strong mind.
They are the pride of the State:
THE DYMO SPORTS CLUB.
They work out, to breed their ideal minds.
 Not like that weakling inferior.
Well, we'll show him.
They wait.

When will the money be again?
 Let them report on this one.
The State is generous.
 But wait!

Listen.
Solitary footsteps on the deserted street.
He is always alone.
That in itself is suspicious.
If he is alone, no one can watch him.
Well, twenty are watching him now.
Twenty superior specimens,
watchdogs for a totally healthy society.

Here he comes.
Just like him.
Always alone.
What can he be thinking, if he is always alone?
Nothing good, we grant you that!
Damn him.
His arrogant solitary footsteps pacing by.
Well, twenty pace out behind him.

Block after block.
He walks on, steadily.
He must know what's coming.
Arrogant damned bastard!
They walk faster.
He walks on.

At the door,
their fates eclipse.
A punch, a kick.
Many kicks and many punches.
Kick after kick and punch after punch.
There go his glasses.
Stamp them out, then his eyes.
Break his fingers.
The left hand! The left hand!
That's the one he uses!
The right one's for salutes!
Kick him! Punch!
Out of the way! Here's mine!

Don't kill him!
A dead writer is no writer at all!

Six months in the hospital,
that's what they said!
Six months, no more, no less!
There!
That'll show him!
Damned, bloody heap!
Some superior specimen now!
One turns, to spit.
Our signature.
Not like yours!
Let's go, boys!
Back to the basement room of health!
We've done enough tonight!

Long live the State!
All hail to the cash box!
A toast to superiority!
Makes a man feel good!
Makes a day!
A glorious day!

In the beginning
was the Word,
they say.

Well, in the end, was the boot,
his end,
HAR! HAR! HAR!

THAT
WHICH
RESISTS

Brett Rutherford

IN PRAGUE, A TREE OF MANY COLORS

for Jan Palach, Czech martyr,
who set himself on fire January 16, 1969
to protest the occupation of his country

I am born, I am sown.
I am screaming as the sun tropes me out of the earth.
I am dragging in my tendrils the hopes of spring,
I am pulled, exhorted into summer. The light
deceives me with its deaths and resurrections.
I must be straight. I must not believe
the mocking sun and its revolutions.
I must wait for the ultimate paradise,
the world's light redistributed for all.

Much passes beneath my shadow:
crowds press to marriages and funerals—
the upright grooms go in,
the silver-handled caskets come out,
the church, the state, the people
move on in soot and sorrow, day to day.

Why do these people whisper always?
Why do so many avert their eyes from me?
Why does neighbor spy on his neighbor,
 reporting every oddity to the men in black?
Why do I hear the rumble of thunder?
Why does the symphony break off?
Why have the women gone to the cellars?
Soldiers and tanks are everywhere!
The streets are full of Russians and Poles,
Hungarians, Bulgarians, East Germans —
all of East Europe has come to crush us!
Men with fur hats speak swollen, Slavic words.

Death is here. The smell of blood is here.
My roots touch the entrails of the hastily buried.
Anger is everywhere. I hold my leaves,
make camouflage for lovers, conspirators.

Students rip down the street signs
and hide them in my upper boughs—
the invaders drive in circles
and cannot find their destinations.
I open my bark for secret messages,
encourage pigeons to carry the word
of where is safe and who is betrayed.
Here comes that student, Jan Palach,
the ardent one, the solitary dreamer.
He stuffs his coat with my fallen leaves,
fills his cap, book bag and pockets with them.
He is the icon of our unhappiness:
he will open like a triptych of gold
into a flame that will embarrass the sun.
When he exfoliates in gasoline
I am with him, burning,   burning,
leaf by dry leaf   exploding for liberty.

Brett Rutherford

THE EXHUMATION OF GOETHE

Weimar, Germany, 1970

By all means do this at night, while Weimar
sleeps, while even those whose job it is to watch
the watchers, sleep. In merciful dark,
the third shift silence when the local electric plant
shuts down for the Good of the State,

take a cart — no, not a car,
    a hand-drawn cart —
dampen its wheels so your journeys to,
    and from, and back
to the foggy graveyard are soundless.

Do not awaken the burghers!
Here are the keys
    to the wrought-iron gates —
mind you don't rattle them.
The crypt has been purposefully left unlocked.
You need but draw the door.
The cart will just squeeze through
(Engineer Heinrich has measured everything!)
Open the sarcophagus as quietly as possible.
Watch the fingers! Don't leave a mark
on the hand-carved cover.
Be sure it's Goethe, the one with a "G."
We don't want his crypt-mate Schiller
(too many anti-People tendencies there).
Lift up the whole thing gently.
The bones will want to fly apart.
Only the shroud, and some mummified meat
keep him in the semblance of skeleton.
Just scoop the whole thing up,
and into the cart like a pancake.

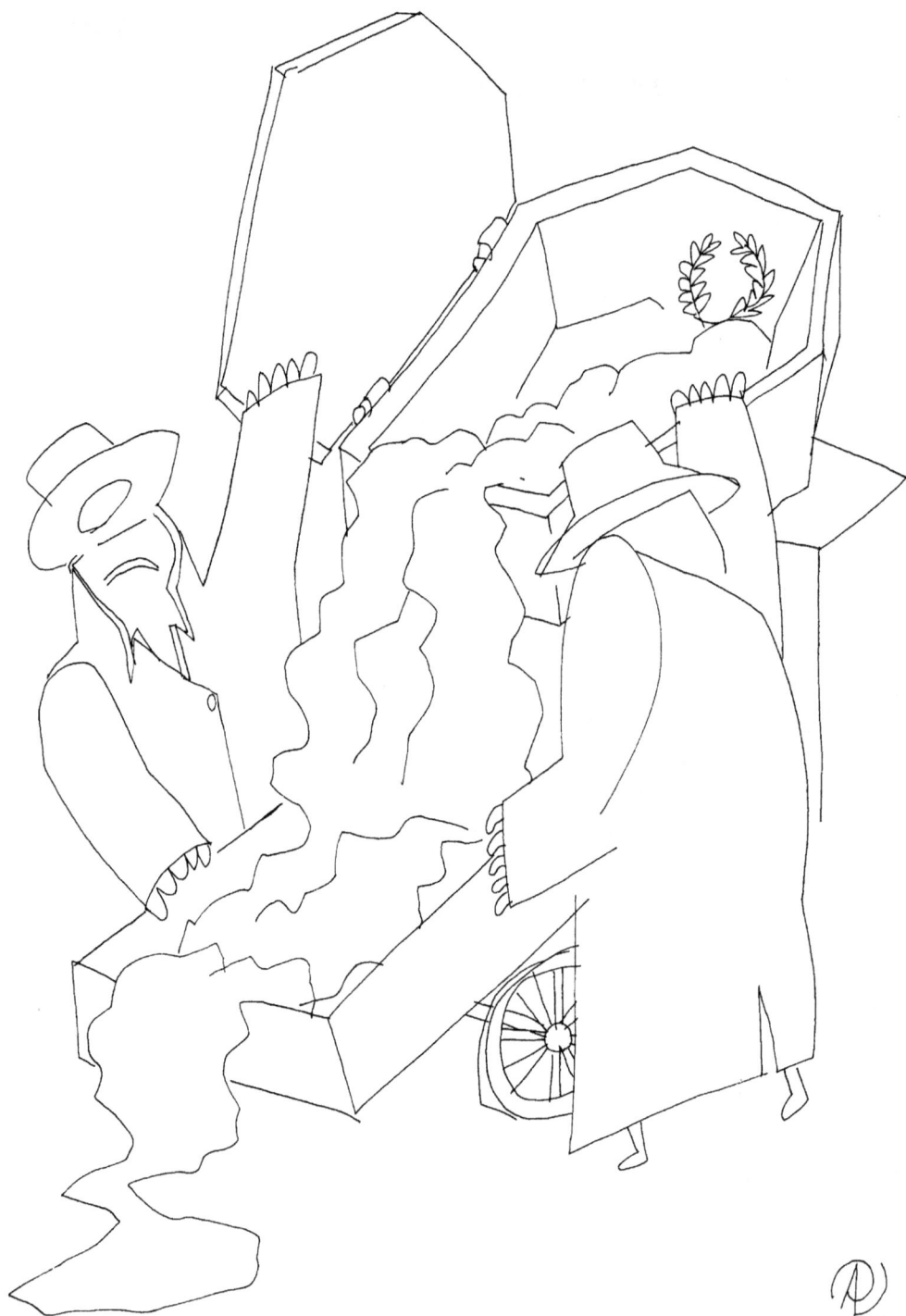

24465

Here's a bag for the skull. Don't muss
those ash-gray laurel leaves.
We plan to coat them in polyester
after we study that Aryan skull
whose brain conceived of Faust,
Egmont and sorrowful Werther.
We're going to wire the bones together,
strip off that nasty flesh,
maybe bleach him a little,
make a respectable ghost of Goethe.

Who knows, if he looks good enough,
in a relined sarcophagus,
we could put him on display.
Come to *Kulturstadt*!
See Goethe's body!
Even better than Lenin!
(Can we say that?)

We'll pipe in lieder and opera.
Tour guides will be dressed as Gretchen.
Maybe a fun house
nach Mephistopheles,
and sausages at Brander's Inn.

Ah! the cart is here! The bones,
yes, the bones. Unfortunate, the odor.
We can work on that.
The colors, mein Gott,
(excuse the expression)
they will not please —
over there, Klaus,
    if you're going to be sick —
It's such a *little* skeleton —
was he really so short?
The books said he towered
over his contemporaries.
So much for the books!
And the shroud — that color —
not at all what we imagined.
Perhaps the opera house
could make a new one.

No, the project is cancelled.
Poets are just too — flimsy.
Next time let's exhume a general,
Bismarck, the Kaiser,
someone with a sword and epaulets.
Armor would be even better.
The People want giants!

Pieter Vanderbeck

EULOGY IN MEMORIAM THE LAST MAY DAY PARADE EVER*

Dedicated to the Republic of Lithuania

All boos have been rehearsals for the Big One.
The Army of Catcalls has risen in the Eastern West.
The better side of a year the armaments had been sharpened.
Then the most miserable day of the year drew up to schedule.

Red Square was empty in its characteristic monolithic ominosity;
yea, even more so, for soon the tanks would roll.
Not conquering grim tanks, but happy celebratory ones.
Lined behind the wall on height-adjusting boxes,
the leaders would take satisfaction in their works.
Not only tanks! Great big rolling cradles boasting their beloved:
rows and rows, file and file, of incubatored aerial exploding
missile warheads nursed on grudge and paranoia,
       greed and sadism!
Ranks, platoons, companies of compliant obedient troops would
       goose-step proudly by,
displaying brandished firearms with mounted knives of bayonets,
heads jerked to the side on passage by the magic painted Lenin!
All was rehearsed, all scripted:
when the people would cheer,
when the people would cry,
when they would joyously sing
new ballads drafted by committees,
when and at what and how would they vent their rage,
and of what they would boast in building-shaking
       communal chants.
All taken care of.
Always taken care of.
In the new revised edition, even before the birth of time.

---

* The failed Red Square May Day parade of 1990.

There was uneasiness, to be sure,
for spectres loomed on all horizons.
The auroras of resurgent life —
not a good environment for mould.
Saint Elmo's Fires waved as bellwethers,
heralding gremlins to worry the Kremlin.

Morning congealed and crowds appeared.
Populace from corners all assembled in their mass.
Brass was polished for mighty chords.
Drums were tuned for corporate heartbeat.
World events may hang in tatters,
but, oh!, what glory in a parade.
Even statues of Lenin might walk.

And indeed, the parade did come.
As fine a parade as ever!
All Important People were lined behind the wall,
their hats in an even row, looking down benignly
at the world they had created.
Youth groups of young conformists marched by,
singing songs of their passionate willingness
to sell their parents to the State.
All armored vehicles drew out from their garages,
to greet the cherry-blossom bird-song Spring.
Here came the missiles! All pointed starkly to the sky.
The drone of diesel engines crawled the cobbled ground.
Parade, parade, parade after parade,
band and tune, all of them,
each one exquisitely official!

But then: what's this?
Ah, yes, the Dissidents!
Granted space this time, to show that they are Russians too!
Signs and placards: ah, ho-hum.
Only a bit to go.
Most of them were still away,
playing fife-tunes to the lichens,
with echoes rung to hear.
Only a bit, only a bit.

But, what's this?
Great big crowds, all Dissidents!
Why, is the land itself a Dissident?
Do the Rocks and Air make trouble?
Earth and Water the Police annoy?
Dissidents! Dissidents! Nothing but!
Signs as many as missiles,
slogan for a slogan,
fists and faces, faces and fists!

Yes, Comrades! The end of the parade at last!
Say "Comrade" one more time,
then spit.
A toast upon the earth:
Mother Russia's suffering earth.
Then walk, to say you are.
Chant, to say you feel.
And cry, to see the idols broken.
Bread will greet the sunlight.
Hope will meet the dew.
Blades of grass will wave amid the bumblebees,
and memories will be revived.

Upon the anvil of humiliation and pain, grief and despair,
was hammered the will to make the future from the past:
what had really always been,
destroyed the trolls of theft and lie.
Time, itself, grew short of humor,
till mountains turned and sighed.

Brett Rutherford

THE PIANO UPRISING

A Dream, from the Dark Years of Poland

1
Troops at the border; all weapons are confiscated.
    Advisors in place, an abundance of secret
police. The informers are always willing.
The Church, pretending everything, doing nothing,
locked in the stasis of state against god,
the people's servitude a foregone conclusion.
The men are drafted into the army.
The miners and workers uneasily obey
the order to stay at their critical jobs.
The women wait in endless queues,
    their shawls and kerchiefs aligned
like segments of an endless tapeworm
    kept at the edge of hunger.
The meager stores can barely feed them.
The cattle and chickens and eggs go East,
    get eaten by the well-fed army,
        leaving a handful of dwarfish cabbages,
        the ubiquitous potato, the accusing spaces
        of emptiness on the collective's shelves.
Women work in the steaming kitchens,
    coaxing soup from skeletons,
    bread from rye, a bottomless pot
    of cabbage ends and sausages. Somehow,
        everyone eats.
They put aside an extra helping
    for the buxom and blond granddaughters.
At night, or in slices of stolen afternoons,
    youthful and agile-fingered,
girls master the dancing of eighty-eight steps,
play on thousands of legal pianos —
the old Mazurkas, the Waltzes, of Chopin.
No one has thought to outlaw the instruments.
As Nadia practices in Gdansk,

Lidia plays grandmother's spinet in Krakow.
A school piano in Warsaw
    hums by itself in resonance.

No one knows they play to one another,
that the Polish girls have long ago ceased needing
to guide imprinted keys in their études.
No one suspects they are secret weapons,
    strings drawn taut,
      brass frames like crossbows.

Determined and sinister, shining and black
    as coffins in a showroom,
they bide their time rehearsing
    the *Revolutionary Etude* for the people,
    the *Marche Funèbre* for the martyrs,
roulades of Paderewski held in reserve.

The police think nothing of the white-haired tuner —
he goes from home to home, adjusts,
    restrings and tempers,
adds unusual parts to the pedals.

An abandoned piano factory springs to life,
new models in crates on the loading docks,
the shipping manifests immaculate.
It seems that everyone is getting a piano.
The Minister of Finance shrugs. The economy
opens an eye and goes back to sleep.
The Minister of Culture smiles:
music without words is a harmless
expression of the people's art.

2

Nadia practices in Gdansk.
In Krakow her grandmother's
	piano is waiting.
In Warsaw the instrument
	she studied on
	hides in a cellar
	(the piano underground).
Then From a million radios
a great C resounds,
	eight octaves thick,
a *Resurrexit* of brass and wood,
a rhapsody of unity,
harmonics to the *n*th degree.
Casters unlock, wheel guards
	are thrust aside.
Grands roll through empty apartments,
	tiptoe impossibly
	down curving stairs.
	Spinets swerve out
		from alleyways.
Baby grands dart
	from tree to tree,
play cat and mouse
	with the traffic police.

The sergeant leafs through
	reports of abandoned furniture,
scratches his head in puzzlement.

It is, of course, the piano rebellion.
The pianos are coming:
	wheeled piano tanks
		death black, coffin-shaped
	polished and retrofit
	with well-tuned armaments.
They all play Chopin in unison —
the *Military Polonaise*.

Their lids drum open and shut like jaws,
rolling on tractor tires, juggernauts
rumbling bass notes, the *r-r-r-rum-ta-tum*
of Polonaise audacity.

The battle begins:
Pianos crash from the rooftops.
A phalanx of interlocked pianos
take the field, soundboards locked
    in invincible wedges.
Flying pianos buzz over the airport,
   their black and white teeth
    rat-tat-tat arpeggios,
down with ease the clumsy MIG fighters.

They drive the generals into the sea.
The troops desert,
    lock arms and dance
    into the countryside.
File clerks toss documents from windows,
    topple file cabinets,
    pour chicken soup on bureaucrats,
sing *r-r-r-rum-ta-tum* in the hallways.
Cornered in public squares
the secret police deny everything,
their crimes, their ranks, their names.

In Warsaw the sweating minister
of secret police and internal security
shouts on his hot wire to Moscow:
"Not royalists, stupid, *royali*, pianos!
it's an uprising of legions of pianos.
Tell them — tell them the pianos are coming!"
The connection is broken by a piano wire.
Instruments regather in the countryside.
Flying Becksteins invade Soviet airspace,
lead missiles cat-and-mouse
back to the planes that launched them.
(Whoever thought a hammerklavier
could turn right angles at Mach 2?)

The Polonaise goes on.
Others conduct guerrilla war
to the shifting beat of Mazurkas.
Lithe and supple assassins
hunt down the Russian advisors
(those white enamel spinets,
fast on their wheels,
eager to leap from a third floor window
to squash a fleeing foreigner!)

Steinways roll through Warsaw,
    Polish flag on their sides,
Bösendorfers to the rescue at Lidice,
Baldwins at the border to reinforce them,
Becksteins fight shoulder-to-shoulder
    with lowly domestic models.
Antique pianos in square cases
come apart at the joints but fight;
half dozen harpsichords at the windows,
    watch wistfully.
Their quills fly out like arrows.
A tiny virginal bursts its frame
    to whip a visiting professor of Marxism,
draws blood with snapping steel wires.

The highway is clogged with black Volgas.
Battalions of Russians fall back in retreat.
And this is but the start of it:
As Anna practices in Leningrad,
Irina plays grandmother's spinet in Moscow.
A school piano in Odessa
    hums by itself in resonance.

Pieter Vanderbeck

TWO FIGURES

One trudges through the snow.
Flakes fall around him.
There are some pine trees.
He leaves a row of tracks behind.

He has something on his mind.
He has something of a mind.
He thinks of planets and death.
He also thinks of fate and music.

He looks behind.
His tracks dwindle into the haze.
But in the direction they suggest
there is a distant standing figure.

He has seen it before.
He trudges on,
welcoming the thickness increasing,
wishing a wind to cover his tracks.

The other has one purpose:
to follow him,
note his every movement,
assemble a file.

What he thinks,
what he says,
who he is,
to whom he speaks.

Always the same distance behind,
always there somewhere,
amassing a biography
that can be an indictment.

The great eye sees.
Nothing can escape it.
What it thinks
is known to none.

VISA GRANTED, WITH GRAVEL

Enough
    polite letters to the Ministry
Enough
    waiting for the refusal of visas
Enough
    bread-dry mornings for the good of the state
Nothing
    will stand between him and Freedom
Nothing
    but the wall that entombs Berlin from the sun
Nothing
    but a little barbed wire, a
    handful of guards with tiny bullets,
    the frown on the face of the portrait of Lenin
Nothing
    but a guardhouse pin-pocked
    with bullet holes, dusty macadam
    rust-stained with fugitive blood
Nothing
    but gravity prevents him from leaping over
    but inertia prevents him from charging through
    but brick and stone-

If the wall is an immovable object,
    he must become an irresistible force.
One truck
    cargo his girlfriend
    his eight-month-old child
One truck
    piled high with proletarian gravel
    seven tons weighted to the limit
    all but the needed gas siphoned away
        to prevent explosion
    turned into a high-speed ram to test
    Newton's laws against the state's

One truck
    hurtling toward gates like a reckoning
    outspeeding the reflex to aim and shoot
    breaking through wood at Checkpoint Charlie
    breaking through bricks at Checkpoint Charlie
    breaking through concrete for the dream of —

The astonished guards fire at the juggernaut —
    one shoots to miss and thinks Lucky bastard
    one shoots to kill because no one
        should escape the People's Paradise

A hundred miles of brickwork tremble
as the seven ton passport crashes through.
Another hairline crack mars the perfect wall.
The East shrugs and transfers
    the files of two workers
to the black cabinet marked *Former Persons*.
Though someone else will have his room, her place
at the University, friends repeat their names
with reverence, as though a transcendent world
had lifted them into the clouds like saints.
It is this:
A letter to the editor. A report to the Western press.
A polite petition. A week in the anteroom
of the Ministry of Refusals. A guest suite
in the Hospital for Maladjusted Workers.
Or this:
A truck with smashed headlights and a crumbled hood.
A load of gravel. Eye to eye
    with captors and guards,
foot to the floorboard at last doing something
weeping at coming out alive, shouting for joy

breathing the free air on the other side of the wall

BORDER GUARD

Now and then, a man whose job it is to shoot
his fellow citizens, enjoys a day at leisure.
He does not go to a crowded cafe. The dreary
bleached faces on television annoy him.
The films and books he would like to see
are forbidden, the satire plays closed down.
He walks down streets that have forgotten
their names, opens a twisted gate and walks
into a ruined cemetery. He likes it here.
These people died before the bombs,
    before the chapel became a shell,
      when the living had time to honor the dead,
        the patience of stone carvers
           to mark their passing —
      when the living had space to house them
        each in an individual grave —
not the quick, anonymous flame of cremation
    nudged from behind by the next in line.
These trees were planted before he was born.
    No one nails slogans to them.
    These crows are not informers.

A shard of stained glass falls to the ground:
a saint's eye, a halo chip, a puzzle
piece of a forgotten benediction.
An acorn descends, a leaf
tears away from the structured tree.
Why should one leaf among its classless brethren
defy the order and symmetry of oakdom
to make its assuredly fatal plunge?
The acorn must fall,
the squirrel must do his duty
and bury it. Even a new oak
that springs unintended from its sepulcher
is doomed, each tree
another jailhouse, a jabbering asylum under an iron sky.

But a leaf — a leaf has a chance —
a wind might catch it, a bird
might seize it from an updraft
and carry it to freedom.
Who knows what becomes of one *over there?*
Maybe an anarchy of leaves, maybe
a touch-me-not defiance of order,
maybe they plant themselves
on any tree they please —
oak and ash and willow and holly,
the plane and the pine,
a jostle of maple and cedar and birch —
melting pot trees in a jigsaw forest —
or maybe a peaceful wood, each uniform tree
striving its best toward the eternal light? —

Why should one man, fed and provided for,
his job assured, his humble bed, his state-
assured cremation — why should one man
cry *nay* against the law-compelling land,
to burst through the checkpoint
        where *he* was trained
to shoot at any outlaw breakout, to stop
the spy, the saboteur, the secretor of wealth?
He thinks of the truck that barreled through,
of the joy and terror on the driver's face,
how he had fired to miss, thinking *Lucky bastard,*
how his comrades had failed to stop the seven
ton juggernaut, how no one really wanted to.
He knows of dozens of failed escapes, knows
the bloodstains, the bullet holes, the patches
in the length of the hundred mile wall.
On the other side there are wreaths for those
who died trying. "Did them a favor,"
the sergeant boasts. "What would they do
in the decadent West anyway? Nothing but drugs
and poverty. Nothing but trouble."

Next day, the sun beats down accusingly,
a fusion-powered torchlight, soul-baring.

He walks to his station like a criminal,
fears the secret police could read his thoughts,
like banners hung from a dirigible.
He takes his rifle and rounds,
his heavy coat and helmet, assumes his place.
His stern reflection in the guard post glass
fools no one — he is a frightened boy:
tired of this game, these dullard playmates,
this oppressive school. He drops the gun,
slides out of coat and helmet, turns with
a voice not quite his own and says to the guard beside him,
"Comrade, what if I crossed
the checkpoint now — what if I walked
right into the West — would you shoot me?"
His companion's face locks in agony.
"You didn't say that, comrade. I didn't see you.
My gun —" he smiles — "My gun could jam."

He waves to the guards on the other side.
He takes a breath. He runs
and no one fires a shot behind him.

Where an oak leaf trembled and fell
a piece of sky now admits the blue
of the alter heavens. The leaves are astir.
They don red jackets for their breakaway.

Where once a guard stood resolute,
a question mark settles like a gull,
a dare replaces a salute.
The guards are all investigated.
The sergeant who assigned the guards is demoted.
The lieutenant in charge of the sector
is brought before a loyalty board.
The army considers more robots and dogs.
Along the wall, the stones themselves
shift in their mortared places and ask
Why are we here?

THE
MONOLITHS
FALL

Pieter Vanderbeck

GENIUS OF THE CARPATHIANS

The last Communist flees through the countryside.
His overcoat is so fine.
The people have let him down.
They did not believe in him.
So much he did for their own good,
and this is the thanks he gets.
He should have done more.
If only he had known.
Discipline! that's the key.
That's where they all failed.
His brothers under grass,
where projects could have been.
A dream failed.
He runs.
Every headlight is a danger.
Every crossing to be avoided.
No place to hide!
Where are they?!
Nothing but people!
No masters. The cold settles in.
He is hungry.
Oh, what glory he had.
And the people, too!
It was their glory.
And there would have been more!
Glory upon glory!
He hears the music still.
A light down the road.
He dives into a ditch.
Oh, his wonderful coat!
Trumpets, thousands.
Anthems to spare.
But now, only the crickets.
They are looking for him.
A billion eyes.
His people.

His ungrateful people.
If only he had known.
He would have done better.

A voice.
Yes, calling to him!
At last!

"Here I am!
Your glory!
The architect of your happiness!
The scientist of your ideology!
Come, embrace me!"

What is this?
A glare?
A gun?
And pointed at him!?

"Remember?
Don't you remember?
I am Prometheus!
I provided all!
I invented programs!
I steered the helm!"

Of what?

"'Why ... why ... the State, of course!
Yes, the State! And the people!
And history, destiny, the future!
Why .. .! steered everything!
Oh, my child: you are lost!
Come, help me!
Embrace me!
Glory can still be ours!
Yes, you too! A bread.
Some warmth.
Some water.
A change of shoes.

A place to sleep.
What's this?!"

Only the muzzle of a gun.
His gun!

"Remember? I made that gun."

It does not help him.
He is carried off,
remembering music.
Great symphonies.
Rows and rows of granite.
Inspiring granite.
He goes into the night,
as the country flounders helplessly.

What will they do?
They need me!
"Get me to the Capital!
No, no, not that way!
Do you know who I am?"

The wind blows through the weeds.
The rocks rest beneath the moonlight.
The people are still there,
and so is the nation.
The dead can rest.
Their time is won.

Brett Rutherford

WINTER SOLSTICE 1989

December skies are ominous:
gray walls of cloud
obscure the universe.
Even the sun is secretive,
a burnished coin
in miser's pocket,
a hooded monk,
a bashful Cyclops
now in, now out of snowstorm,
avoiding the north like a criminal.
Whoever thought that such a sun,
such arctic wind blasts,
could herald liberation?
Who knew what anthem
   the wind blasts bellowed,
what symphony the arctic snows
had scored on skytop?

Joy, thou source of light immortal...
Beethoven's hymn
   and Schiller's ode
played by an East/West orchestra,
sung by a chorus
eager to substitute
Freiheit for *Freude,*
a burst of happiness
sparking from Bernstein's eyes
as he conducts them.
"*Freiheit* indeed," he says,
"and not a single bullet was fired!"

Crowds fill the public squares,
shake fists at balconies.
In Hungary the People's Party
abolishes itself;
wire cutters make souvenirs

of barbed wire barriers.
In East Berlin they planned to shoot
protesters, crush their placards
beneath the wheels of tanks:
the generals depose the leader.
Dumbfounded border guards
read orders to let all citizens through,
protest to newsman:
   "This means no job for us!"
Hole after hole, gate after gate,
the hundred mile barricade shatters.
Guard towers fall like dominoes.
Two Germanys embrace and weep.

Daughter of Elysium...
In Prague, the workmen knock down
a neon hammer and sickle
from the local power plant.
In Poland, the workers remove
the frowning bronze Lenin
no longer managing
his bankrupt shipyard.
The Russians who once
gave tanks to crush rebellion
now tell the Czechs
they'd better reform — and fast!
The aged leaders in Belgrade,
encrusted lords of Sofia,
tremble and surrender rule
to the astonished populace.

In Bucharest they spit
on portraits of Ceausescu,
whom but a month before
they eulogized
The Danube of Thought,
Genius of the Carpathians.
Soldiers beg
for a place on the firing squad,
load and fire

before the order is even uttered.
It takes three days
at the blowtorch
until the frowning monolith of Lenin
   the king of workers
      in his suit and vest
   dainty fingers
     that had lifted no tool —
   falls to the jeers
    of the crowd.
A flatbed removes
   the humbled colossus,
cheek to the ground,
his exhortative gesture
meaningless.
The workers chant
no *Internationale*.
His bronze should crack
to hear their anthem today:
No more Communists!
No more
   Communists
     ever!

The boot has lifted
from the face of Europe.

Pieter Vanderbeck

A NEW WORLD

What does it mean,
    for Lenins to lie on their side,
ready to be crated,
carted off in trucks?

A world with no horizons
hiding darkened sides,
not to east or west a building looms,
windows nonexistent, dungeons many.

In the stillness of an evening breeze,
no lurking 'round a corner, waiting hidden
can be felt or sensed or smelt,
and walking, talking, can go on the same.

Without an enemy beyond our border,
the enemy within is impotent,
no longer free to bargain off
one side against the other.

Without a healthy rampant fear,
the grimy cloud of terror no longer can survive,
but must avoid both man and sunlight,
for fear it might become undone.

Therefore, let the banner flutter in the breeze,
of stripes of colors symbolizing
lands of rocks and trees,
lakes and mountains, clouds and airs.

Brett Rutherford

IN THE STREETS OF MOSCOW AND ST. PETERSBURG

Idol-smashing multitudes, I salute you!
    Cut off Lenin at the kneecaps,
        then lift his noos'd neck
           at the end of a wrecking crane.
Topple Dzerzhinsky from the KGB he built.
How imperious he looked in his bronze overcoat,
now nothing but a tumbled derelict!
Marx's face is daubed with splotches,
    red paint, white paint — his imperium now reads
WORKERS OF THE WORLD, FORGIVE ME
Prostitye menya ... prostitye menya ...
The dying words of Boris Godunov!
Do not stop at these beginnings,
O Russians long suffering!
Rip that filthy mummy from Lenin's tomb!
Scatter the bones of Stalin to the dogs!
What to do with all the toppled monoliths?
Melt them down for bells!
I hear new bells in Moscow tolling,
Low the notes, melancholy the harmonies.
Bells of iron, bells of bronze
Bells of the sorrow of a million kulaks.
Bells to shatter the walls of Lubyanka,
topple the last towers of bitter Gulag.
Ring them all in one great universal chord!
Let the largest orchestra ever assembled
play the Overture of 1812!
Cannons bursting! Fireworks over the onion domes!
Swing the clabbers! Lenin's head is a church bell!
Stalin's a row of jolly carillons!
The brow and beard of Marx intoning
Glory! Glory! *Slava! Slava!*

Pieter Vanderbeck

THE BERLIN WALL

THOUSANDS HAVE TAKEN TO THE STREETS.
TENS OF THOUSANDS!
HUNDREDS OF THOUSANDS!
A FRACTION OF A MILLION!
DAY AFTER DAY,
WITHOUT A BREAK.
GOVERNMENTS HAVE STIRRED AND TREMBLED.
POLITBUROS HAVE BEEN PURGED.
THEN,
THE WALL HAS OPENED.
TWENTY-EIGHT YEARS,
TWO MONTHS,
AND TWENTY -SEVEN DAYS;
BUT NO MORE! PIECES ARE TAKEN APART,
GIVEN AS GIFTS,
SOLD AS SOUVENIRS;
WHILE THE GUARDS STAND BY,
STARING AT THE DANCING CROWDS ATOP IT.

EVEN IN THE FREE WORLD,
THERE IS CONSTERNATION AND CONCERN:
COUNCILS ARE CALLED,
ANALYSES ARE SPECULATED:
WHAT DOES IT MEAN?!
WHERE WILL IT LEAD!!?
CAREFUL BALANCES IN THE FREE WORLD
ARE SUDDENLY UPSET.
IS THIS A NEW TIME?
IS THE WORLD TRULY SICK OF TYRANNY?
WILL FREEDOM BECOME ABSOLUTE?
WHAT WILL THIS DO TO THE ECONOMIES!?
WHAT WILL BECOME OF THE BALANCE OF POWER??!!
THE PRESIDENT SENDS HIS CONGRATULATIONS;
BUT HE WORRIES.

THERE ARE SO MANY BERLIN WALLS!!
WE EACH HAVE BUILT ONE FOR OURSELVES!
OUR ECONOMIES HAVE DEPENDED UPON IT.
WHATEVER WILL WE DO NOW?

WHAT CAN YOU DO WITH A GAP IN A WALL??
IT IS NOTHING!!
YOU CANNOT GRAB IT!
ALL YOU CAN DO IS GO THROUGH.

Pieter Vanderbeck

ERSTER TRINKLIED

I sing to you, von Bismarck;
I, a German, drunk on brew;
superior brew, superiorly drunk;
I sing this gross mess,
a poem I composed;
yes, a poem, for you;
not guns rammed up your ass,
but pretty lyric verses,
laurel leaves upon your iron tomb,
cooing white doves perched upon,
stirring, fluttering,
dropping droppings as they do,
phosphorus upon the granite,
there soon to be rained upon,
nourish plants within the earth,
daisies on your grave,
from all the doves that perch upon the ramparts,
battlements, of Prussian city's monuments!

I sing to you,
I sing to you,
disgusting pickled drunk with brew,
as evening settles on the frigid streets
of this cold mean and crafty city!
A poem!
A poem!
Why, a poem?
You, the iron man?
Why this scribble literature?
Because, because,
this is what you ended.
You see?
I sing upon the end
of what you started.

Germany, its many kingdoms,
left the world
when you, my leader, took control.
It is with you, director, friend,
that Germans became a hated race,
became a race at all!
How many years?
Six score minus one!
Seventeen times seven!
It is with you that pens were melted down
and hammered into swords!
Hammer, hammer!
Helmet, shield, and spear!

And even here, composers walked the streets.
Writers drank their coffee,
artists read their papers.
All of that was long drowned out
by thundered stamps of marching feet;
and wood and marble passed away,
to brass and granite, iron, steel!

But now, a Germany begins again;
not with blood, and not with iron,
but with a multitude of common people's hands,
grabbing, tearing, down a wall;
defying passports, guards, and dogs,
falling to machine gun fire;
motivated by a common will:
to get out, to get out,
to get away, and not come back again.

I sing, I sing,
a drunken slob,
saying what I think,
no title to my name,
no consequence in what I say;
just noise I make,
in dewy settled night,
while headlights beam upon the road,
and strollers happen by.

I sing because I'm German,
my hands not red with blood,
but black with powdered carbon,
making many lines
of words and pictures drawn upon the parchment.
I sing because I enter history,
the history of thought,
the history that wins with charm and logic,
the history that people pay to hear,
my carbon over steel!

I wave my pen,
and have another brew.
By morning, I will drink my coffee,
read, and write again.

Brett Rutherford

WHAT'S IT TO ME

What's it to you? a neighbor asks me.
Why write about Germany, Poland,
 the struggling masses of Russia?
Who cares? We're all Americans now.
Why you of all people, with that fine English name?

English is but part of what I am,
and even that is outsider,
Northumberland and border Scot,
three ancestors beheaded
at the Tower of London,
rebels against the throne,
so don't imagine me
on the Queen's Christmas list.

As for the maternal side
count me a Theobaldus
    Thibault in France
    Diebold in Alsace —
Vosge mountain village
from which we heard the call
to serve Napoleon
    and answered
(young Diebold a water boy
at the Emperor's own tent).

We fled Alsace
to escape the Prussians
    who killed an old woman
    for calling a *kartofel*
    a *hard apfel*,
traded the sweet Vosges
for the wild Appalachians

Cousins back home
    endured the Prussians,
    celebrated reunion
      with France,
    and then endured the Nazis.

All the young men of Alsace
    were drafted for infantry,
sent to the Eastern front.
Most died, but thousands
    were captured.
They never came home.
Unwilling "Germans,"
they died in Stalin's gulag.

Oh, it's personal.

MILLENNIAL WINDS

Pieter Vanderbeck

ORODRUIN

A new wind is blowing in the East:
the stronghold of evil has crumbled,
the shadow has lifted.

The chimes of the new year
ring throughout the solar system,
returning a song that began an age.

The time of iron is broken.
The idea has dispelled the physical.
The imagination is president.

This is a call for an unending war,
with horrors surpassing to face;
and it has begun.

All who think and dream are to stand,
to pursue the criminals who use instruments to fight,
to the very last one at the farthest longitude.
This planet is free!
It joins the universe in its history.
The living and the dead.

The word breaks open walls,
the line releases prisons,
the cadenza topples power.

A new proclamation, a new term,
this earth is at a turning point.
Never more shall bullets battle evil.

Bullets are extinct.
Weapons belong to a buried age.
The earth has left the physical.

Ring in a new year,
that will reclaim the lost ones,
the voices of the dead will say!

Culture reigns, its prime minister Humor.
long times and trials we will face together.
The boundaries of our nations melt.

Ring the bells of every land.
A time, a decade, century, indeed, a future!
To the end of time itself the bells will ring.

Brett Rutherford

SARAJEVO DOLLHOUSE

"All over the city sheets of burned paper, fragile pages of gray ashes, floated down like a dirty black snow. Catching a page you could feel its heat, and for a moment read a fragment of text in a strange kind of black and gray negative, until, as the heat dissipated, the page melted to dust in your hand." — (Dr. Kemal Bakarsic, librarian of Bosnia's National Museum, describing the burning of the National and University Library, 25-27 August 1992).

Let's play. It's Sarajevo 1992.[1]
A nice old European city.
Here's a doll house, a fine
old building near the urban center.
Artists and musicians live here,
to be near the concert hall,
the Conservatoire, the theaters.

But something has gone amiss.
The front wall,
which we, as gods,
were accustomed to opening
so we could examine our dolls,
is gone, blown to a thousand
shards and smoldering cinders.

Amid the tumbled chimneys,
the shattered slate of rooftops,

---

[1] **Beginning in April 1992, Serbian nationalist attacks on Bosnian cities and towns deliberately and successfully targeted national libraries, museums and archives, in the process wiping out nearly the entire written record of Bosnia's history.

Among the losses is Bosnia's National Library in Sarajevo, which also contained the university's holdings and the country's national archive of newspapers and periodicals. Prior to its destruction, the National Library held over 1.5 million volumes, including 155,000 manuscripts and rare books. It was bombarded for three days with incendiary grenades on August 25-27, 1992, and was reduced to ashes.

a broken piano lies upside down
and cannot right itself.
A French horn has melted,
into a grandfather clock,
its twisted face now telling
not time, but terminus.
A writer's desk has leaped
onto an awning, loose
sheets of an interrupted epic
up and out on the wayward breeze —
the doll pages are tiny as postage stamps
and in their updraft they meet
the downward fall of burning paper,
ash glowing on text as the letters
burn hotter than the space
that framed them.

Why did the dolls not run away
when the nearby library exploded?
The exposed rooms tell all:
how the dreamers, the writers,
the mad ones with all the operas in them
refused to leave despite the danger.
"No one – not even a Serbian –
would bomb the library, right next door."
A grandmother doll ,
white-haired in her rocking chair,
teacup and silver platter beside her,
listens to Bartok on tiny headphones —
listens forever, and her eyes are gone.

The room above, the garret
where we left the hungry poets
to their own devices last time —
(Rodolfo and Mimi from *La Boheme?*)—
is still a wild tangle of lovers' limbs.
but they are all asunder —
two heads locked in a melted kiss,
pairs of legs and arms
under the sheets at impossible angles,
a single foot cut off at the ankle,
four shoes at the door, going nowhere.

The gaunt violinist who looks
ever so much like Paganini,
sits in his underwear rehearsing —
fiddle to chin and left hand
fingering a great arpeggio —
the arm with the bow
is nowhere to be found.
The dramatist is in the other garret.
His fountain pen is raised, his eyes
look up in astonishment — words cannot say —
his legs have run off without him.
Mock crows pick at his leg bones,
amid the branches of the mock plane tree.

Our doll house has fared better
than those of our neighbors.
The dolls' University is a shambles,
some pyromaniac child
burnt up the libraries – just walls
remain, an outer shell
surrounding an ash pit.

The acrid smell of burnt
plastic fills the air —
toy soldiers consumed,
along with toy firemen,
nurses and local police.
There's even a Mosque
with a burnt-up little Imam
and little singed prayer carpets.

But all is not lost.
We manage to gather
a dollhouse orchestra
and send it to play
in the library ruins.

We thank our stars
that none of this happened
in the larger world,
that the child with matches
has been punished,
that the melted, shattered
denizens of our house
can be replaced

with new ones.
No harm done.
No one would bomb
a library,
a museum,
a concert hall!

Pieter Vanderbeck

BLOOD AND IRON

Since the earth congealed,
iron has stood against iron;
both have raised a flag.
One has prevailed:
the iron of the sword.
One has flowed into the earth:
the iron of the spirit.
One has been forgotten: the iron that remained.
One has lived, and will live always:
the one that is remembered.

Let the swordsman swing,
let the marksman aim,
let the tractor treads of tank battalions roll.
They can have their money,
they can eat potatoes,
and they can die.
For time is but a minute,
and death is final.
But honest blood will never die,
as long as legends can be told.
The whole world listens
for a fallen people;
and in the end,
blood will rise again,
until, as the Sun burns to a cinder[2],
blood is all that's left.

And from its germ
another universe will start —
planned upon the old,
its blueprint: memory.

---

[2] When a star dies, all that is left is a core of iron.

Pieter Vanderbeck

THE DEATH OF COMMUNISM

A dragon has died.
Its blood seeps into the porous earth.
Its last gasp has been heard.
The blackest and the hollowest of its malicious shadows
has reared its nimbus to propose eternal horror,
then on a wind borne from memories of sunlight
has blown away to whimpering inconsequence.
The dead rejoice.
The tortured weep.
The ruined cast their blessing to the air.
A vampire, great, with many offspring, darkens the earth no more.
Its few remaining children tremble, seeking crevices to hide.
Let life begin.

Brett Rutherford

AS IDOLS FALL IN THE AFGHAN HILLS

The Taliban destroy historic Buddhas in Afghanistan

What to do?
What to do?

Mail a Mullah
a thousand portraits
of Bodhisattvas.

Airdrop a hundred
thousand little Buddhas
on tiny parachutes
onto the streets
of Kabul.

Mate giant Japanese
Buddhas with Godzilla,
send their offspring
to the Afghan Hills
to sit serene
in lotus pose

(but watch their fire-breath
melt Taliban tanks
and send the soldiers
shrieking!)

Skywrite
LORD BUDDHA
from border to border
in every known language.

Or wait for Karma
to burn the burners,
shatter the shatterers,
silence the mouths
of the speakers of law?
(No time, no time
as the dynamite explodes
a Buddha head
from fifteen hundred
years ago.)
Let Allah, Buddha
Christ and Brahma
rage like comets,
moth fluttering
around the Man Sun.

One vanity makes them,
A greater vanity destroys them.
Yet a child with hands in clay,
in the mud by the riverside
will make a new god
with broad shoulders
far-seeing eyes,
a forgiving visage,
a palm extended
for the benediction
of unbearable Beauty.

This parched land
needs its memories,
its slender share
of human fairness,
against the dark night
of goats and dynamite.

Pieter Vanderbeck

AT THE BORDER SOMEWHERE
IN THE MIDDLE OF GERMANY *

Remember when we were the East and West,
and each encroached upon the other?
Now we are between the East and West,
and both encroach upon us both.

Remember what terror a doorway held,
and a certain vertical rectangle held a dreaded figure
come to visit, take one of us away,
assassinate the other?
Now a rectangle is a rectangle,
that we can walk through either way.

I will tell you what ideology is!
It is drinking beer and eating bread,
and going to evacuate.
My signature is what I water in the woods,
upon a frosty morn the warm steam rising up.
My corollaries are yawning in the morning,
my amendments a snore beneath the moon,
my articles a grunt and a turn,
my amendments are a snuff of nosy snot!
My constitution the nitrogen cycle,
my anthem the phosphorus cycle,
my title the carbon cycle,
my Marx and Engels hydrogen-hydroxides.
That's ideology enough for me!
I think I'll go and take a pee!

---

*On the completion of the dismantling of the Berlin Wall, and the opening of the Brandenburg Gate.

Pieter Vanderbeck

THERE ARE STILL COMMUNISTS

There are still communists,
I know.
I see them all the time.
They hurry in and hurry out,
plan mischief, mayhem, injury and pain,
and codify it all to make themselves seem grand.
Everywhere and every minute
are Communists being born,
little babies drooling malevolently,
their phosphorescent venom dribbling on the high-chair tray.
Oh, what they will do when they can talk!
What messages they will carry when they walk!
Their diapers cannot change fast enough!
For they were born to serve a cause!
Well, they are everywhere,
between the rocks and woodwork,
waiting for their hour to come out,
rallying in secret closets to amass a force of arms,
planning things that most will never know about.
I smell them, hear their many feet, a single body carried.
I have known so many! And come to think of it,
am still upon the list!
My children are on future lists,
my ancestors on historic lists,
their whereabouts never known,
        the last life moment the night they disappeared.
I will never know how much they ate,
if any bread or any water,
nor how many lashes they received,
how many years they got,
or what the charges were,
if any charge was written.
All I know: they disappeared,
usually at night, usually alone.
And no one ever asked,
or let concern be known.

Children raised in camps,
not knowing they were born.
The state invented them,
they die but by decree!
Yes, they are still there,
hiding in the corner, watching me,
planning what to do
when they arise again!
I think they always will be there,
until the end of time!

Brett Rutherford

OCTOBER THOUGHTS IN WAR-TIME

What does October mean?
    To the old Bolshevik the month we finally took what was ours —
    to the old émigré the month we lost everything,
    and had to flee to the border.
To the Spanish and Portuguese, Italians and Greeks,
taking café in treeless plazas,
the aftermath of equinox, a few brown slurries of oak leaves
skittering from Alps to the sea, not a time, but a passing,

To the Chinese, a mottled dream of maple, gingko,
ailanthus and willow, in which one pale
and angular scholar, his beard as thin as an artist's brush,
takes tea in his gazebo, as the autumn's white tiger
runs down the bounding deer.

For me, in this New England city,
it is not quite autumn.
I spy the moon's new crisped crescent
hovering above the Hopkins house.
An angry Mars is at its nearest —
all these heavenly bodies tugging at treetops.

The Unitarian bell tolls eight, as Uranus,
a dim flickering, grazes the steeple
as though curious to know
for whom the clapper sounds the bronze.

The weary earth has had enough explosions.
Winter will yield up autumn,
if autumn will erase its merry carnage.

If leaves do not fall, perhaps the heads of state
will leave decisions   undecided,
prisoners un-decapitated,
toxins unmanufactured,
uranium un-enriched —
perhaps the deadly elements
will go unmined, the gray bombers
unmanufactured,

the hateful thought, snug in its walnut,
from its high branch
unfalling.

Pieter Vanderbeck

ST. PETERSBURG

*On the popular vote to rename Leningrad as St. Petersburg,
restoring its original name.*

Restored, is the Golden Eagle;
Silver, Copper, platinum feathers,
tail of Nickel, Mercury eye;
Iron in its beating heart, and Lead as it remembers.

Let the Tin of ringing bells
proclaim its voice across the atmosphere,
from mountain range across the plain:
active once again, the Metals stand!

Jewel of shining brilliance, your eye a beacon glows,
and in the northerly aurora lights the nighttime sky.
At the great divide where meet a pair of mighty watersheds,
stands the Diamond crowning Russia's Destiny.

St. Petersburg, the name an invocation
of years gone by and years to come,
memories before memories, sights beyond horizons,
a name that ringing bells on speaking peal!

Pieter Vanderbeck

WHAT WILL HAPPEN TO LENIN?*

Comrades!:
What will happen to Lenin?!
Who wants him?!
Where will he go?!
The building is coming down!,
Or turning to a restaurant!
No more a reviewing stand!
His place is needed!
He's being at last kicked out!
No rent, no tent!
Shall we put him in the ground?
Shall he nourish flowers?
Who will give the plot?
The party has not dough to buy one!
Does charity raise a hand?
Does memory?
Nostalgia?

Do you not miss that knock on the door?
The electric air of sustained terror?
The structured line of ideology?
The warmth of the factory party cell?
The squint of the knowing secret agent?
The railroad to Siberia?
Shall we send him where your family is?
Kolyma? Verkhoyansk? Fahrenheit minus ninety-two?
Freeze him in the permafrost?
Sell Lenin steaks and Lenin cubes?
Comrades!, He deserves an answer!
He gave you all an answer!
What answer will it be?

---

* On the toppling of Soviet statues of Lenin, and the possible closing of the Lenin Mausoleum.

Comrades!, We must act!
The landlord, he is coming,
in his hand a writ,
the other hand a fist!
The landlord comes on many legs,
and wears out many shoes!
He has many writs to serve!
Upwards of five thousand!
We cannot merely burn him!
Can we?

Pieter Vanderbeck

OLD STATUES NEVER DIE

Iron Felix rusts away,
the red of blood to orange and yellow changing.
What once was the symbol of unyielding might
colors the earth in hydroxides.

Granite Felix stands presiding,
father of a thousand terrors,
one hand showing, the other hidden
as the ropes around are bound.

On the base the old inscription
has all been obliterated.
What was it? I can't remember.
Something like, "I close my talons,
lovingly with death caress you."

Wooden Felix stands on the shelf,
a smaller replica beside him,
on the other a larger one,
an apt shell to fit in
with compounded uniformity.

Off to the park of heads and figures,
some lying on their side,
heads at angles quizzically viewing each other,
as children and pigeons walk between.

Meanwhile, Walter Ulbricht walks across the Platz,
on his way to the crypt of Willi Stoph.
A typical ice rain is falling,
glazing many granite and bronze surfaces.

They will confer over empty glasses
on the dull routines of eternal materiality.
Forget the thousand years!
They cannot die.

As the idea lives, so the statues must walk.
Even with their names forgotten,
hands and ears lying broken in gardens and roadsides,
heading purposefully in the first direction they are turned.

Close the windows, draw the curtains,
when you hear the iron pacing,
granite, copper, marble pounding
on the round uneven cobbles.

Brett Rutherford

THE TWENTIETH CENTURY

We thought the world would end.
We thought the world would end.
     It didn't end.
        We ended.

TNT uranium   hydrogen neutron
cobalt strontium   mushroom clouds —
those megatons   were mega-nothings.
Our sleepless nights the averted nightmares
of Holocaust and zombie aftermath.
Shelters and radiation suits,
clickety-click-click of Geiger doom,
roaches inheriting our empty cities.
These didn't happen. But the earth's doom
sits in missile-tip submarines,
ever flying bombers, subterranean launch holes
to the delight and profit of various cartels

But we began to die anyway.
The least minds of our generation
adrift in the poppy-coke ecstasy-grass
hallucinogenocide snort-shoot-smoke death derby
to the delight and profit of various cartels
or we stumbled sleepless
in shopping mall airport Times Square
shilling Bibles or Vedas or Mormon blather,
getting clear with Scientology,
drinking the Kool Aid in Jonestown,
or calling the fat old Korean
munitions maker the honest to God Jesus Two
to the delight and profit of various cartels

or we loved one another to death,
became pestilent walking skeletons
in our holy orgy cities
New York and San Francisco,
and the dregs of medicine
experimented upon the poor
to the delight and profit of various cartels

We thought the world would end.
We thought the world would end.
        It didn't end.
                We ended.

Pieter Vanderbeck

THE GHOST OF MAY DAY

When the ice melts to the mosses,
a sweetness rises in the still-crystalline air,
fresh earthy vapors rise from the pungent soil,
winter retreats to the layer of permafrost,
small meadow flowers open their colored buds,
in the gentle breezes an atmosphere of elation is felt,
it is then, during the opening of gold-green leaves,
that the wide central square of granite cobbles
is cleared and cleaned for the great annual celebration.

On one side will stand the great masses of all people,
on the other, in a row on boxes behind a balcony,
shoulder-to-shoulder in symbolic solidarity,
the leaders watch the passing.
First the troops, their rifles ready,
an ocean of them, marching in synchronized strides.
Music of brass and drums to shake the earth.
Then the tanks, their cannons pointed upwards,
as wide as the square, synchronized fumes of petrol rising.
Then the flat-cars with the missiles,
pointing upwards as they should be,
each one a mushroom cloud to outnumber all others.

The square shakes.
The world has eyes to see.
All hold their breath and tremble.
No doubt who can make the most fallout.

Now the wind across the empty square blows,
grasses waving around the reviewing stand.
The tanks are in their garages,
being cannibalized for spare parts.
The missiles do not fire when they should
        or do when they should not.
There are no uniforms for the soldiers,
no pay, and no food either.
But the earth still shakes,
and fear trembles jelly-like in the remembering air.

VETERANS' DAY PARADE

The peg-legged cats of New Bedford
march with the handicapped mice,
Half-worms and headless mantises,
ransomed from the mouths of robins,
barely keep up with the centipede marshal,
hobbledy-hob on thirteen braces,
twenty-seven legs shy of a hundred.

Pairs of one-winged bats fly tandem,
an air show of squeaking somersaults.
Singed moths and poisoned dragonflies
careen and smoke like wounded biplanes,
sky-writing dyslexically
the place-names of recent battles.
A buzz-huzzah rises from the float
of wingless flies (playthings
of wayward boys or of a vicious god).

There is a war on, but still
the parade limps and staggers
to amputee drumbeats
and fingerless fluting,
one-lunged horn calls,
snaggle-tooth riffs
abruptly voiced and just
as abruptly silenced.
Foot, feeler, stump and tentacle,
cane, stick and crutch
time-tap the slow march,
the Dead March, the *Marche Militaire*,
wave after wave of the wounded,
proud of their medals.

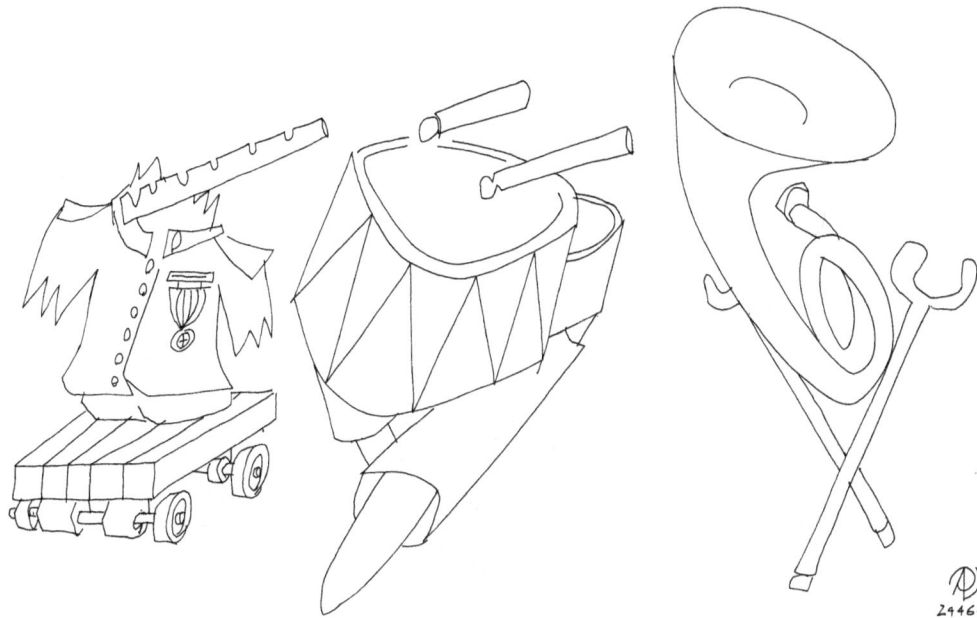

The blind bishop, a miter'd mole,
waits at the bandstand.
Though deaf, he will bless on cue,
to cornets and drum rolls,
as the gulls, in chorus, incontinent,
take aim at the generals' helmets.
Wheelchairs and walkers snap in salute
as the bishop raises,
     on the end of his hand-hook, the trans-
substantiated Host
assuring them all of eventual reunion,
     (after the Victory)
with their missing body parts.

Pieter Vanderbeck

GROWING UP WITH MUSHROOM CLOUDS

There was Mickey Mouse.
his synchronous circles we can never forget,
even less than a three-leaf clover.
Then there was the swastika —
the evil one, that is —
and that is still around.
But there is another,
and we see it everywhere.
Some who do not know the shape of the Earth,
recognize that.
    The Manhattan Project,
    Bikini Atoll.
    Hiroshima.
    Nagasaki.
We saw them everywhere.
News stands.
Movie theaters.
Television sets.
Even commercials.
They were made into rubber stamps.
Poor children carved them out of potatoes.
They were scribbled in notebook margins.
They were easy to draw.
And why shouldn't we?
We!
Children of Plutonium.
We,
who have not known a clean Earth.
We,
who wallow in a world-wide film of fallout.

Little grains of alkaline metals
do we wash, drink, eat, and breathe in.
Meanwhile, those of the Most Powerful in the Power Industry
proliferate plants to produce the plethora
of the actinides in all their isotopes.
We are the transuranium generation,
our shapes the mushroom cloud and the cooling tower,
and don't forget friendly Mister Atom, beneficiary of all.

Brett Rutherford

AND THEN WE GOT USED TO THE ATOM BOMB...

We thought the world would end soon.
We huddled for omens: nightly
    the television spoke disaster —
sat by a faux-log fireplace
    that burned but was not consumed
with pipe-smoking professors
whose worst-case scenarios

    high-altitude detonation
    firestorms   hyperheated steam
    plutonium half-life   millennia
        of runaway mutation
    universal death, sudden only
        for a minority,
        but for the majority
        a slow torture of disease
        *and disintegration**

filled our waking dreams.

The men who know the most
    *are the most gloomy.**

Somehow their worried wives
    afraid to bring more children
    into a nuclear winter
saw their way to garden and cook,
raise their soon-to-be-cindered
boys as though, somehow,
it would all come out in the end —

an explosion of blond energy
    played all around us,
model airplanes aloft,
    their bomb-bays open —

in their world, pilots returned,
    bombs were recovered
    from the carpet pile,
       the cat's fur,
    reloaded, re-used
on ever-renewing enemies.

We listened to Bertrand Russell,
    on a well-played record,
    reading his latest warning,
    co-signed that fateful year
    by Einstein on his death-bed.
"First we had the atom bomb,"
the Englishman intoned —

    —the plastic airplane darts again —

"and then we got used
    to the atom bomb,
and so we developed
    the hydrogen bomb."

    —an even bigger bomber model
      descends from tiny hands —

Shall we put an end to the human race
    *or shall mankind renounce war?**

    and an ice-cream truck melted
    somewhere in Japan in mid-
    tune, while children
    with rising sun nickels
    danced into chrysanthemum
      fireballs —

It is too late, he said,
    to be invoking god —
    the god of bullet holes
    and amputated stumps
    and useless dead.

It is too late, he said,
    to be waving flags —
what color blood and honor?
which side of civil war,

    holy war, muddled
ideology, can claim us?

So Russell and Einstein said,
as simple as sunlight,

*Remember your humanity
and forget the rest.*[3]

I came to tears upon those words —
the danger all too real
that these small boys
would be bombed — or bombers.

Strange, they are grown now.
The world did not explode,
    but not for lack
of military effort.

---

[3] Lines in italics are exact quotes from the Russell-Einstein Manifesto, July 9, 1955.

PRESIDENTIAL UPDATE

Deaths down in Iraq! Yes, really!
Only a thousand killed this month!
This is progress.
Four hundred thousand weapons
have gone missing, admittedly,
but as the NRA can tell you,
guns don't kill people,
people kill people.
Last month we obviously succeeded
in killing the people
who killed everyone the month before.
Now that's a good policy:
kill everyone who kills anyone,
except, of course, us.
Next question, please —
       not you, not you,
       not you, not *you* —

Pieter Vanderbeck

FAREWELL TO EARTH

My heart sinks for the ground I stand on,
the honest, noble Planet.
Man has defaced It for as long as he could move on land,
but now, he has done it,
all and forever.
The Air is of a different composition,
causing changes in weather patterns.
The water is befouled and undrinkable,
poisoning and killing its contents of life.
The land is covered with sewage and garbage,
and seeped with industrial toxic waste.
People live longer, but maintained by machines,
spending half their lives with newly discovered diseases.
Major blocks of insect species, reptiles, birds, animals, plants,
disappearing by the decade, knocking out food chains.
Industries, governments, banks, failing and falling apart.
More radiation every day, all over the Earth,
as transuranium elements are produced and stored.

In time there will be no sweet wind to waft through forests,
no shimmering crystal lakes of delicate rising mists,
no cries and twitters of birds in the morning and evening,
no beauty of Nature remaining in pockets,
only a barren waste-strewn desert,
a lifeless Planet whose only sound is empty wind.

THE PROPHET BIRD

Answer to Pieter Vanderbeck's "Farewell to Earth"

I have heard the shrill call of your prophet bird.
Night and the moon have brought me out
to the sea shore to hear its funereal song.
I will not weep, cannot despair.

I stand on this storm-blown, sea-rising
drought-ridden planet, yet my heart
is not sinking, even as maniacs
wild-eyed and waving Kalashnikovs & holybooks
explode themselves and bring carnage around them,
even as I consider Europe a vast boneyard,
the Middle East a trash heap of uncivilizations
    piled high since the first silt of Nile & Tigris
    gave idle kings & priests the criminal idea
that they, or their supernatural betters
had dominion over everything, and for all time.
What creatures! Fashion a stylus or a horn of brass,
and then a scimitar. Invent polyphony,
then make for Torquemada
an exquisite device for torture.
Should such vile animals,
    with the table manners of Harpies,
be written off by the Animal Kingdom,
turned out by thorn and briar by the Plants,
poisoned to extinction by acrid Minerals,
blotted by the very sun and stars?

I answer only that Beauty redeems everything.
Even the tiger, when it is not hungry,
    looks on the bounding gazelle
    as a thing of wonder.
For the line of one neck and shoulder
    on a Phidian marble,
one phrase of Handel or Mozart,

one heart-stopping dab of paint on canvas,
we are forgiven much. We share with life,
    from pseudopod to mammoth,
    from the most delicate tendril
    to the great bulk of whale-flesh,
the way the all-too-familiar disk
    of the sun-faced daisy might see us,
the fascinated horror we feel
    as we regard the self-
        illuminating eye of the giant squid —
all monstrous to all, all beautiful to all

as long as life goes drunk on self-delight
    and aches for the touch of its kind,
as long as we know that all life enjoys
    the benediction of earth-turn and sunrise
that the first word the Universe uttered
    was *Surprise!*

Another human chapter is ending.
It is not the end of everything
    (only the thin-lipped prophets
    with their dry-leaf Bibles
    believe that everything will end).
The story is not over.
It will never be over.
Walls and guard towers have fallen,
    death camps and prison camps closed.
All this is good. That some mass murderers
    sleep in their pensioned beds disturbs me.
That new Lenins and Berias and Stalins
    are waiting to be born, disturbs me.
But life itself has something in store for us.
We will star-leap if we must to another Earth
if we cannot learn from this one.
The air, yes, is a different color now.
Trees on the mountaintops brown in its acid.
If elm, beech and chestnut
    possessed a smiting god to call upon
the green world would rise and smother us.

Full half of the cause of the harm we do
    is that we live so briefly,
so little time for giving and healing
    after so much seizing and taking.
So let us live longer, not less,
    let us become old-timers, undying,
        cyborgs if we must —
if all the great men and women past were there for us,
    even if only as their brains afloat in a tank
    in squawk-voice semblance of living,
still they would come to us
    the way the ghost-Athena seized
        the sword-hand of Achilleus,
            saying to him, *Don't do that*

It is because we die
    that we make Earth an ashtray,
        choke ocean with petrol and Styrofoam.

I do not worry much about banks, and mortgages.
Things fall apart, and pass away.
Their place will be taken by other things.
I would welcome the end of six-lane highways,
the tic-tac-toe of airplanes across the sky.
I see a different millennium unfolding
    not of steel girders and oil derricks.
So long as we escape the total madness
    of mouth-foaming God-told-me-so
        hand-on-Apocalypse men,
so long as our better natures prevail

I will live to see every book ever written
available free to everyone on earth,
Beethoven free, Homer and Virgil and Dante,
Shelley and Poe and Whitman for everyone,
a never-closing museum that all may walk
alone or in the best of company —

Your prophet bird
    would sing disaster,
minor in downward scale —
my bird, the melody inverts,
    beaking the flats away,
    my scale ascending.

HOW THIS BOOK CAME TO BE

Through happy coincidence, Pieter Vanderbeck was my neighbor in the student-infested Fox Point neighborhood of Providence when I moved there in 1985. During the exciting days of the collapse of the Soviet Union and the end of old-style Marxist dictatorships throughout Eastern Europe, we came to realize that we had both been writing, over a span of some two decades, many poems based on the sorry plight of artists, musicians and ordinary mortals in Russia and the Eastern Bloc. Some of the later poems in this book came to pass as we shared news and anecdotes about the tumultuous events in the region.

Many of these poems have been read at open readings here in Rhode Island and in New York City. They have circulated on the Internet, and a few found their way into print in magazines. But most stayed in our portfolios until they were gathered for the first edition of this book in 1992. The anti-Marxist tone of many of these works made them pretty much anathema at poetry readings, and I was screamed at a few times by poets and college professors for the simple act of relating, in poems, actual events related in newspapers. At some of the same readings I heard Russian émigré poets ridiculed, and Solzhenitsyn described as an agent of the CIA (imagine being paid to get cancer and spend decades of your life in the Gulag, just so you could tarnish the image of the USSR!).

I am not a prisoner of ideology, and am equally opposed to Marxist dictatorships, fascist dictatorships, and theocracy. I'm an Age of Reason ethical humanist, atheist, libertarian type of guy, with a streak of anarchism. I'm suspicious that almost anything big in the social or political realm is bad, and if you sent me to Heaven, I'd head straight for Lucifer's jumping-off spot.

When I encountered Pieter Vanderbeck's poems I immediately recognized that here was another mind concerned with truth, values and liberty. Pieter is a Gogol to my Voltaire or Hugo. His poems display remarkable empathy with the victims of totalitarianism, evoking Orwell and Kafka. He is almost a walking catalog of man's inhumanity to man, from Torquemada to Idi Amin. Mistaken for a misanthrope, he is a great sympathetic string to the world's cries for justice. There should be one such on every Supreme Court.

The other theme that binds these poems together is our mutual love for the great tradition of literature and music in Russia, Germany and Eastern Europe. Thus these writings refer to Shostakovich, Solzhenitsyn, Chopin,

Mussorgsky, Goethe, Schiller, Pushkin, and Beethoven as part of our common heritage.

I discovered classical music around the age of thirteen, and found the pursuit of musical knowledge and experience — especially opera — as a gateway into European high culture. I taught myself to read the Cyrillic alphabet at age fifteen so that I could sing Russian folk music and opera. My first poetic smatterings of French, Italian and German also came from hours of poring over opera libretti while listening to long-playing records. Later, as I spent half my adult years in New York City, I grew accustomed to thinking of American and European culture as one continuum. As I met and talked to artists and writers who had escaped from Russia or the Eastern bloc, the gap between the Left's take on these People's Paradises, and the testimony of escapees, seemed jarring.

This book, although it recounts some of the dark days of the 20th Century, is intended to celebrate the gradual triumph of the idea of freedom. The events of 1989, with the fall of the Berlin wall and the disintegration of long-established Communist governments, was surprising to say the least. Even more surprising was the lack of jubilation in America.

This book was not "politically correct" when it was published in 1992, since it served as a reminder of how awful things had been, and a celebration of the vast potentials for liberty and prosperity. This new edition, published in the wake of the Balkan wars, 9/11, and the ascent of American fascism under Cheney and Bush, is again "politically incorrect." Our newer poems take on the Taliban, Serbian incendiary bombing of Bosnian libraries, and the Cheney/Bush war machine. It was also an opportunity to reflect on ourselves as the Atom Bomb generation, and to debate whether, with global warming, we have finally reached a crisis that we cannot fix. In balance, this longer book is an equal opportunity offender of orthodoxy.

Many of the poems gathered here were inspired by specific events.

"Ivan Grozni" is about John Demianiuk, a Cleveland auto worker who was found to be a Treblinka prison guard. After numerous trials and appeals over two decades, he was finally deported to Germany for trial in early 2009.

"Solzhenitsyn in New York," was provoked by an account of the great exile attending a Bolshoi Opera performance in New York.

"Stalin and Shostakovich" is based on Ian Macdonald's biography of Shostakovich and on contemporary accounts of Stalin. I am startled that, at this late date, I still have to persuade some people that Shostakovich was not a loyal Communist.

Pieter's shocking "Brawns 20, Brains 0" is based on events in Rumania documented by Amnesty International. The members of a group called the Dymo Sports Club were paid by the state to beat up writers.

The oldest poem here is my "In Prague, A Tree of Many Colors," originally drafted in 1969. Unhappy with the poem, I did not include it in the first edition. By incorporating more details about the actual invasion of Czechoslovakia in 1968, I was finally able to make this poem say what I meant it to say. Even more information came my way in 2011, leading me to create an even more expanded version of the poem, now titled "The Linden Tree in Prague." This new version is appended at page 127.

"The Exhumation of Goethe" is based on a newspaper account, although all the details are imaginary and satirical.

"Eulogy In Memoriam" is an impression of the failed Red Square May Day Parade of 1990.

"Visa Granted, with Gravel" is based on a news account of an East German young man who plowed through Checkpoint Charlie with a truck full of stones. "Border Guard" is an imaginative look at the border guard who did *not* shoot at the man in the truck.

Pieter's "Genius of the Carpathians" was originally titled "The Last Communist." The original title was misleading, since the poem is clearly about a party boss, not a rank-and-file Communist — in fact, the poet had in mind the Rumanian dictator Ceausescu, one of whose epithets is given in the revised title.

"Winter Solstice 1989" was inspired by a concert conducted by Leonard Bernstein, in which the words of Beethoven's Ninth Symphony were altered, with Freedom *(Freiheit)* substituted for Joy *(Freude)*. The other most poignant event was a concert given by a lone cellist, Mstislav Rostropovich, sitting at the Berlin Wall.

Pieter's "Erster Trinklied" looks backward to Bismarck, and considers the whole horrible legacy of militarism in the German states.

In "Orodruin," Pieter reflects on the success of revolts in East Germany, Czechoslovakia, Hungary and Rumania.

In "Sarajevo Dollhouse" I lament the return to the political map of 1918, and the savage incendiary bombing of Bosnia's main library.

Pieter wrote "Blood and Iron" in January 1991 after the overrunning of Lithuania after its declaration of independence. His 'Death of Communism" was inspired by the failed Moscow putsch of August 1991.

I wrote "As Idols Fall in the Afghan Hills" in 2000, as the Taliban used dynamite to destroy historic Buddhas carved into the side of a mountain. Gate.

"At the Border Somewhere in the Middle of Germany" commemorates the final destruction of the Berlin Wall and the opening of the Brandenburg Gate.

"October Thoughts in War-Time" is an anti-war poem, and it was disconcerting to be back in the anti-war mode, with one's own country as the aggressor.

Pieter's "What Will Happen to Lenin," "Old Statues Never Die" and several other related poems look on the iconography of Soviet-era statues. The shifting politics of Russia have seen statues of Lenin, Stalin and Dzerzhinsky (the KGB founder), toppled, warehoused, moved to public parks, de-commissioned, and re-commissioned, as Russia has fallen under its own alarming wave of nationalism and power-grabbing.

The Vanderbeck poem "Growing Up with Mushroom Clouds" and the Rutherford "And Then We Got Used to the Atom Bomb" betray our age. We were both children in schools where we were sent to basements or air raid shelters in anticipation of Russian nuclear missiles. In my poem, I recall hearing, as a college student, Bertrand Russell's impassioned plea for nuclear disarmament. It is hard to convey to young people today, what it was like when we literally feared nuclear annihilation on a daily basis.

Two very different poems conclude this book. Pieter's "Farewell to Earth" is his darkest poem ever, and does not offer much hope. I was compelled to answer it in my best neo-Transcendentalist, Whitmanesque mode. My final poem here, "The Prophet Bird," is both an answer to Pieter's gloominess, and a celebration of the prospects for 2009, and the hoped-for end of Cheney-Bush alarms.

Tyranny seems to stand behind the mask of every large human undertaking. The large becomes the inhuman; the inhuman becomes the monstrous. Even the poem cannot be trusted. A poem becomes a Holy Text; a Holy Text becomes an executioner's handbook. Yet poems, paintings, dramas, songs and symphonies have the power to keep tyrants awake at night. These poems tread an uncomfortable, self-conscious ground, part dread, part soap-box rhetoric perhaps, and part a Muse-driven thunderbolt on behalf of justice. We must paint the world as we see it, dream of the world as it can be, and hope the rhapsodizing helps make it come to pass. The Holy Fool hounds the mad Tsar to his early grave.

Brett Rutherford
Oct 10, 2011
Providence, RI

THE LINDEN TREE IN PRAGUE

for Jan Palach, Czech martyr,
who set himself on fire January 16, 1969
to protest the occupation of his country

1

Linden in Prague's Museum Square:
I was born, I was sown
of mother and father trees in some forest.
I screamed as the sun troped me out of the earth,
grew slowly in the shadows of tall buildings.
thrust out my blossoms at the hope of spring,
Years passed; I grew protective rings
around me. Exhorted into summer by sun
and the bacchanal of squirrels, I owe each year
millions of leaf-deaths and resurrections.
The solemn students and professors
stride by with dour looks, eyes locked
into the mysteries of Marx and Engels.

I must pretend to stand up straight.
I must not follow the mocking sun
    and its false revolutions.
I must wait for the ultimate paradise,
world's daylight redistributed for all.
I tremble as angry gardeners trim
the arrogant beard-branchlets
that fringe my still-adolescent trunk.
I am all passion and impracticality.
My heart-shaped leaves are on my sleeves
as I greedily drink sunlight, give shade
to those below in blossom-fall, exude the scent
that maddens lovers to *Unter der Linde* mania,
then paint myself in hues of gold and brown,
shedding my currency in one great shrug

as summer ebbs to frost-dawn.
Behaving well, it seems,
is not in my nature, despite those lectures
on dialectics I hear each afternoon
from the open lecture hall's window.

Much passes beneath my shadow:
across the square, crowds press
to bourgeois marriages and funerals —
the upright grooms go in,
the silver-handled caskets come out,
the church, the state, the people
move on in soot and sorrow, day to day.
On one side, Marx and Engels;
on the other, tradition, and just beyond
my line of sight that monument to Huss,
the great religious martyr. Conflict
divides us like the great Moldau.

We have lived through Kings and Empires,
bad governments and good. Everyone seemed
to think it was getting better last year.
But something has changed now:
Why do these people whisper always?
Why do so many avert their eyes from me?
Why does neighbor spy on his neighbor,
reporting every oddity to the men in black?
Why do I hear the rumble of thunder?
Why does the symphony break off
in the middle of rehearsing Smetana?
Why have the women gone to the cellars?
The earth shakes. Soldiers and tanks everywhere!
The streets are full of Russians and Poles,
Hungarians, Bulgarians, East Germans —
all of East Europe has come to crush us!
Men with fur hats speak swollen, Slavic words.

Death is here. The smell of blood is here.
My roots touch the entrails of the hastily buried.
Anger is everywhere. I hold my leaves,
make camouflage for lovers, conspirators.

Students rip down the street signs
and hide them in my upper boughs —
        the invaders drive in circles
        and cannot find their destinations.
I open my bark for secret messages,
encourage pigeons to carry the word
of where is safe, and who is betrayed.
I guess I am guilty of anti-people
tendencies — who would have thought?

Here comes that student, Jan Palach,
he's all of twenty-one, dark-haired,
a delicate face meant for poetry,
though worn by the study
of too much philosophy, too young.
He is the ardent one, the solitary dreamer.
And more: he intends to *do something*.
He and some others have made a vow,
a terrible pact. He will go first.
He is not Jan Huss,
        burned by his fellow citizens
                over the flavor of God:
he is just Jan Palach from Všetaty,
and he will burn in the world's eyes
because of Philosophy
        (Plato's tanks crushed
                the Age of Reason).

I am his unindicted ally.
The winter ground is covered still
with the dried leaves of my autumn,
some damp, some dry and worn
    to little more than vein lines.
He scoops them up; he stuffs his coat with them,
fills his cap, book bag and pockets,
fuel and kindling for his mission.
He is the icon of our unhappiness:
he will open like a triptych of gold
into a flame to embarrass the sun.
He opens the can of gasoline,
and before anyone can stop him,
he explodes into a fireball,
a flaring marionette; he whirls three times
then falls into a curled ball
of incendiary horror.

2
Earth gives him no resting place.
    As mourners gather
in ominous groupings,
the men in black dig Palach up,
cremate his already-half-cremated frame
and send the urn off to his mother.
There, in Všetaty, no one is allowed
to give him another burial.
No graveyard dares take the ashes
    for half a decade.
In Prague, Palach's first grave
is repossessed. The state deposits there
the corpse of a nameless old woman.
On your way now, nothing to see —
just some old cleaning lady's grave.
No Martyrs in this cemetery —
I'll see your papers please.

3
Twenty years on, a crowd will gather
for something called "Jan Palach Week,"
a pretext to take to the streets again,
and one day later,
    the Communist government falls.

Your ashes, Jan Palach, will return to Prague.
I will be beyond returning, for long ago
an angry axe man removed all trees,
to the despair of poets and squirrels,
the better to conduct surveillance
of all the law-abiding citizens.

There, on the spot of his immolation,
a bronze marker, half cross,
    both Catholic and Slav,
lifts out of mosaic'd pavement.
My last root is hidden beneath it,
as leaf by dry leaf, and ash by ash,
my ghost is a receptacle for tears, and memory.
I was there, around and within him.
I, too, exploded for Liberty.

— October 1969, New York, revised 1986,
rewritten 1996; rewritten 2011